How to Create Language Experts With
Literary Terms

Codi Hrouda and Emma McInerney
with Lyle Lee Jenkins

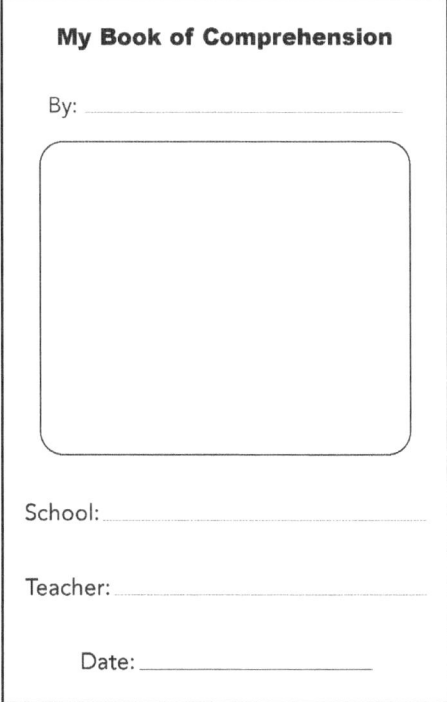

My Book of Comprehension

By: _____

School: _____

Teacher: _____

Date: _____

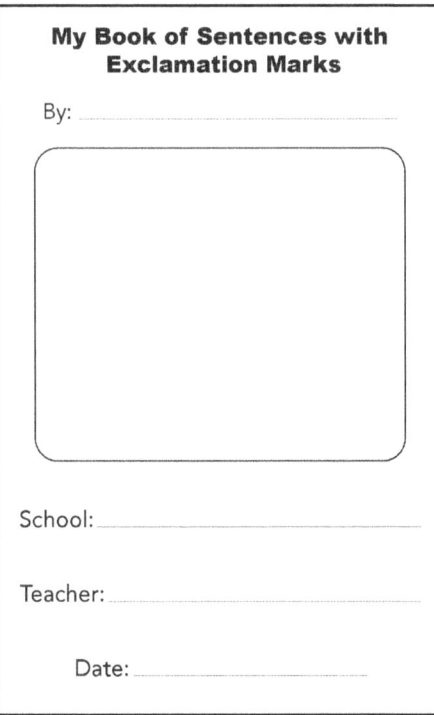

My Book of Sentences with Exclamation Marks

By: _____

School: _____

Teacher: _____

Date: _____

My Book of Rhyming Words

By: _____

School: _____

Teacher: _____

Date: _____

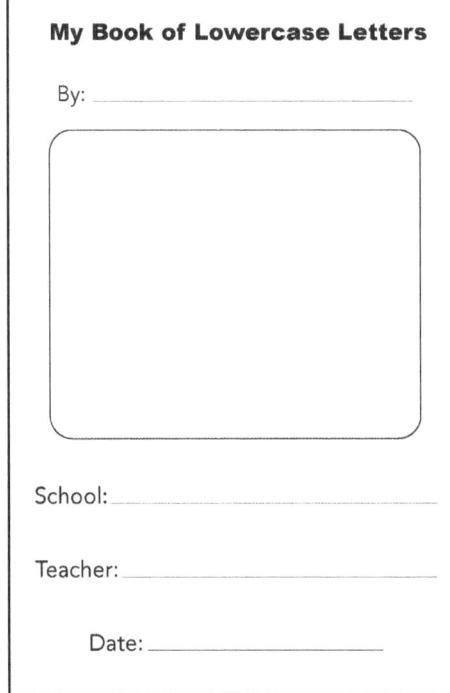

My Book of Lowercase Letters

By: _____

School: _____

Teacher: _____

Date: _____

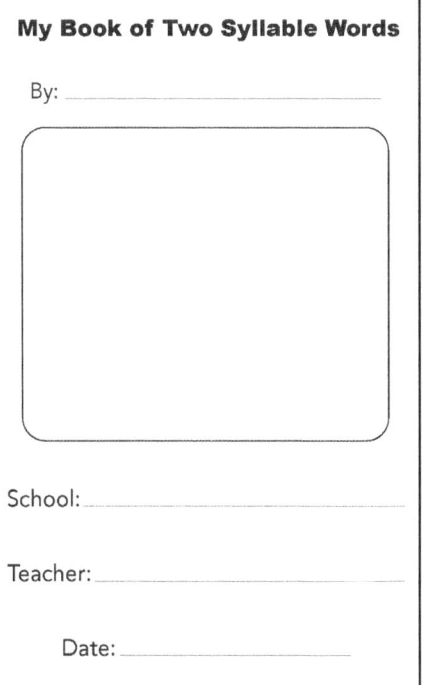

My Book of Two Syllable Words

By: _____

School: _____

Teacher: _____

Date: _____

Perfect School Collection™

To contact the authors regarding keynotes, workshops or bulk orders, visit LtoJ.net/Contact

ISBN: 978-1-956457-65-0

Book Design & Graphics: Christy Courtright, Christy's Customs LLC
Quality Assurance Manager: Kelly Lippert
Publishing Consultant: Martha Bullen, Bullen Publishing Services
Distribution Coordinator: Maggie McLaughlin

Printed in the United States of America

The Perfect School Collection™

How to Create a Perfect School by Lyle Lee Jenkins

How to Create a Perfect Home School by Lyle Lee Jenkins and Kelly Hawkinson Lippert

Perfect School Collection™ Resources

How to Create Math Experts series by Peggy McLean and Lyle Lee Jenkins

How to Create Math Experts with Fluency Quizzes by Peggy McLean and Lyle Lee Jenkins

How to Create Math Experts with Math Standards Quizzes by Peggy McLean, Laura Hayes and Lyle Lee Jenkins

How to Create a Math Foundation for Future Math Experts by Lyle Lee Jenkins

How to Create Bible Experts: Genesis to Revelation by Richard Douglas Junior Jenkins with Lyle Lee Jenkins

Early Readers

Bible Patterns for Young Readers series by Lyle Lee Jenkins

Aesop Patterns for Young Readers series by Lyle Lee Jenkins

Young Authors

Wordless Books for Young Authors series by Jim Chansler and Lyle Lee Jenkins

Special Project

All About Henry: Rich Widower of Savannah Valley by Lyle Lee Jenkins

CONTENTS

INTRODUCTION

The philosophy behind these booklets is that they are student-led, and elementary (K - 6) standards driven. In other words, students can independently complete much of the materials they are expected to learn in school with occasional pre-teaching.

The booklets are designed with a left-brain/right-brain balance. The back cover is a right-brain activity and the inside pages are clearly left-brain. The page prior to each grade level gives parents and teachers background knowledge and suggestions to successfully support their students and children through the booklets.

In order to create and assemble the booklets, parents and teachers can scan the QR code provided at the end of the book to download digital copies. To ensure proper printing, please utilize double sided printing and set your printer to "flip" on the short edge. The front page will be the front and back cover of the booklet. We have also included some bonus booklets within this series to support additional literary term exploration.

Enjoy,

Codi Hrouda, Emma McInerney and Lyle Lee Jenkins

KINDERGARTEN BOOKLET DIRECTIONS

Depending on your student or child's' reading ability, directions may need to be read to them.

My Book of Titles and Authors:
Students will need access to a multitude of texts and coloring supplies. They may need modeling of where to find the title and author on a book cover for this booklet.

My Book of Comprehension:
Students will need to have access to their favorite picture book and coloring supplies. They are given the option to write or tell an adult what is happening in the pictures within the chosen book.

My Book of Sentences with Question Marks:
Students will need to have access to their favorite books. They may need to be pre-taught punctuation and given an example of when to use the punctuation.

My Book of Sentences with Exclamation Marks:
Students will need to have access to their favorite books. They may need to be pre-taught punctuation and given an example of when to use the punctuation.

My Book of Uppercase Letters:
Students may need modeling of how to write uppercase letters on primary dotted lines.

My Book of Lowercase Letters:
Students may need modeling of how to write lowercase letters on primary dotted lines.

My Book of Rhyming Words:
Students may need to be pre-taught what rhyming means and given examples of rhyming words.

My Book of Two Syllable Words:
Students may need to be pre-taught what two syllable words are and given examples/strategies on how to identify syllables within a word.
Example: clapping out each syllable

Student booklets are available via the QR code at the end of the book

Draw your own book cover with a title and author.

_____

_____

My Book of Titles and Authors

By: _____

School: _____

Teacher: _____

Date: _____

Write the titles and authors of your favorite books

Draw your favorite book cover with the title and author.

Titles   Authors

_____   _____

_____   _____

_____   _____

_____   _____

_____   _____

_____

_____

Student booklets are available via the QR code at the end of the book

Draw pictures to tell a story of your favorite memory

My Book of Comprehension

By: _____

School: _____

Teacher: _____

Date: _____

Find four pictures in your favorite picture book and tell a grown-up or write what is happening in each picture.

Picture 1:

Picture 2:

Picture 3:

Picture 4:

Write sentences with question marks:

_____

_____

_____

_____

My Book of Sentences with Question Marks

By: _____

School: _____

Teacher: _____

Date: _____

Circle the question marks in each sentence below:

1. What is your cat's name?

2. I like dogs.

3. Who is taller?

4. When is your birthday?

5. We got ice cream!

6. How old are you?

7. I am two years old.

Copy sentences with question marks from your favorite book:

_____

_____

_____

_____

_____

SENTENCES WITH QUESTION MARKS   9

Student booklets are available via the QR code at the end of the book

Write sentences with exclamation marks:

_____

_____

_____

_____

**My Book of Sentences with
Exclamation Marks**

By: _____

School: _____

Teacher: _____

Date: _____

Circle the exclamation marks in each sentence below:

1. What is your name?

2. We got ice cream!

3. I did it!

4. I do not like cats.

5. Look at me!

6. I am sad.

7. I can ride my bike!

Copy sentences with exclamation marks from your favorite book:

_____

_____

_____

_____

Student booklets are available via the QR code at the end of the book

Draw a picture of something that starts with the uppercase letter. Then write the word using the uppercase letter.

G

D

My Book of Uppercase Letters

By: _____

School: _____

Teacher: _____

Date: _____

Circle the uppercase letters below:

A b C D e f

g H I j k l M

N o P q R s t

U v W x y Z

Write the word in uppercase letters:

cot _____

pin _____

birthday _____

soccer _____

Draw a picture of something that starts with the lowercase letter. Then write the word using lowercase letter.

f

b

My Book of Lowercase Letters

By: _____

School: _____

Teacher: _____

Date: _____

Circle the lowercase letters below:

B p x Y r u

Q s I M c I N

e A f I H k t

R o z G E a

Write the word in lowercase letters:

DOG
- - - - - - - - - - - - - -

BED
- - - - - - - - - - - - - -

CATFISH
- - - - - - - - - - - - - -

KINDERGARTEN
- - - - - - - - - - - - - -

Student booklets are available via the QR code at the end of the book

Write a list of words you know, then write a word that rhymes with each of them.

Words   Rhyming Words

_____   _____

_____   _____

_____   _____

_____   _____

_____   _____

My Book of Rhyming Words

By: _____

School: _____

Teacher: _____

Date: _____

Draw a line to match the rhyming words.

Cat   Cry

Dig   Cup

Mop   Mat

Dog   Raincoat

Up   Fog

Sailboat   Big

Butterfly   Hop

Fill in the missing letters to make a word that rhymes with each underlined word.

<u>Set</u>

G e __

g   t   w

<u>Bad</u>

S a __

d   s   k

Student booklets are available via the QR code at the end of the book

List the names of your favorite songs and circle those that are multi-syllable words.

_____

_____

_____

_____

My Book of Two Syllable Words

By: _____

School: _____

Teacher: _____

Date: _____

Read each word and write the number of syllables it has:

pen ____   rocket ____

helmet ____   capital ____

let ____   picnic ____

name ____   hop ____

basketball ____ napkin ____

Read a book and write any two-syllable words you find

_____

_____

_____

_____

_____

CONTINUE CREATING LITERARY EXPERTS

BONUS BOOKLETS

A quick internet search for literary terms brings up hundreds of words. In addition, there are many topics to study as students gain more meaning from language and increase their writing skills.

Thus, the following blank pages are designed for students to write additional booklets about literary terms not included in *How to Create Language Experts with Literary Terms*. After selecting a new term, students select the format that best fits the task of writing about the literary term or concept.

There are times when children become so engrossed with a particular term that they want to make their booklet larger. These blank pages can also be used to add to existing booklets included in *How to Create Language Experts with Literary Terms*.

Student booklets are available via the QR code at the end of the book

My Book of _____

By: _____

School: _____

Teacher: _____

Date: _____

_____
Title of Book 1

_____
Title of Book 2

Student booklets are available via the QR code at the end of the book

My art:

Student booklets are available via the QR code at the end of the book

Book 1 Title: _____   Book 2 Title: _____

Book Title   Book Title

Student booklets are available via the QR code at the end of the book

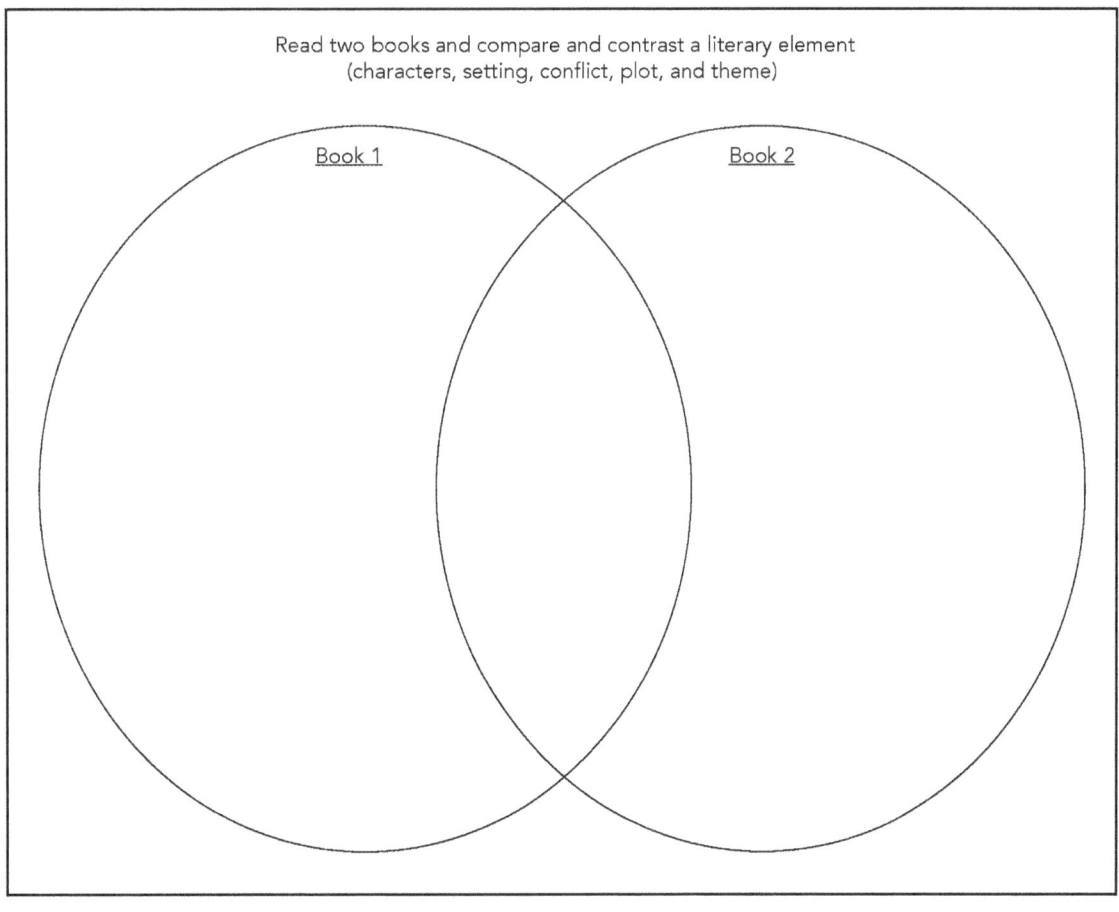

Read two books and compare and contrast a literary element
(characters, setting, conflict, plot, and theme)

Book 1   Book 2

Student booklets are available via the QR code at the end of the book

Book Title

Book Title

Title of Book One

Title of Book Two

Student booklets are available via the QR code at the end of the book

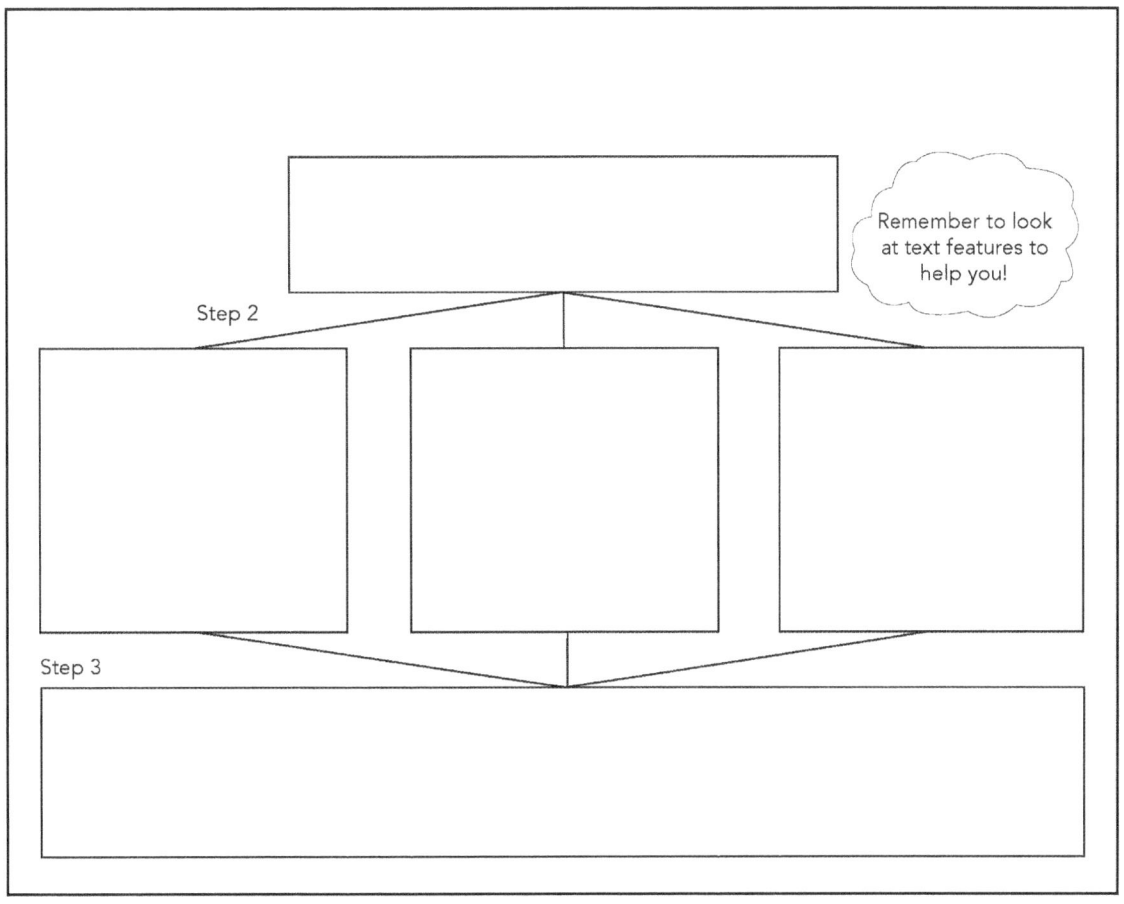

Step 2

Remember to look at text features to help you!

Step 3

Student booklets are available via the QR code at the end of the book

STUDENT BOOKLET DOWNLOAD

Purchasers of **How to Create Language Experts with Literary Terms** may use this QR code to download booklets from this book at no extra cost. This will ease the process of making copies for students and expand learning options. Both the print and digital download versions of this material are protected by copyright laws.

QR codes can be found in all LtoJ books, providing access to digital downloads of student worksheets.

ABOUT THE AUTHORS

Codi Hrouda grew up in the small town of Hubbard, Nebraska. After completing high school, Codi went on to pursue her degree in Elementary Education at Wayne State College, and graduated with a BA in Elementary Education in 2000.

Once graduated, Codi accepted her first job at Thurston Elementary School, in Thurston, Nebraska, as a fifth and sixth grade combination teacher. A year later, she and her husband moved to Columbus, Nebraska where she taught a year of first grade and then thirteen years of fourth grade at Centennial Elementary School. While teaching full-time in Columbus, she completed her master's degree in Curriculum and Instruction through Wayne State College. She graduated with her master's degree in May of 2006.

In 2014, Codi and her husband moved their family back to the area where she grew up to raise their three daughters. Codi accepted a fifth grade position at Dakota City Elementary in Dakota City, Nebraska where she continues to teach today. She just completed her twenty-second year of teaching in 2022. Codi spends her free time attending her daughters' activities, decorating, reading, and spending time with her family and friends.

Emma McInerney grew up in the small town of Elk Point, South Dakota. After completing high school, Emma went on to pursue a degree in healthcare at South Dakota State University (SDSU).

In 2015, she realized she was ready for a career change because her passion lies in education. She transferred to Dakota State University (DSU), earned a degree in Elementary Education, and graduated in 2019. Emma began her first job at Dakota City Elementary, in Dakota City, Nebraska, as a fifth grade teacher. While teaching full-time she completed her Masters degree in Curriculum and Instruction through Wayne State College, graduating in May of 2022. Emma concluded her third year of teaching in 2022, and she continues to teach alongside her co-author, Codi Hrouda.

Emma returned to her hometown of Elk Point after graduating, and spends her free time reading, gardening, and spending time with her boyfriend, family, and friends.

Dr. Lyle Lee Jenkins is an author, speaker, and recognized authority in improving educational outcomes. He believes that implementing a growth mindset and celebrating progress are the keys to helping students learn more and retain their enthusiasm for school.

His education experience, that spans over 50 years, ranges from working as a teacher, a principal, and a school superintendent in the California School System to being a University Professor. In 2003, Lyle Lee founded LtoJ, LLC hoping to impact and guide the way we approach education.

Lyle Lee Jenkins has authored six books showcasing continuous improvement in schools, including *How to Create a Perfect School*, *Optimize Your School*, *Permission to Forget*, *From Systems Thinking to Systemic Action*, *Improving Student Learning*, and *How to Create a Perfect Home School*. All literature offers powerful, practical suggestions for every aspect of education. The two most influential people supporting Dr. Jenkins's work are W. Edwards Deming and John Hattie.

Having spoken to educators all across the United States, Latin America, Europe, Australia, and Asia, Lyle Lee Jenkins is passionate about equipping the next generation with a true love of learning.

Dr. Lyle Lee Jenkins holds a Bachelor of Arts degree from Point Loma Nazarene University, a Masters of Education from San Jose State University and a Ph.D. from the Claremont Graduate University.

Lyle Lee Jenkins's website, www.LtoJ.net, is a great place to discover useful tools to guide your educational journey.

Do you have a great photo or video of your student using one of our products?

We would love the opportunity to share it on our website and social media channels!

Email us at info@ltoj.net

If you have a story to share, we would also like to hear from you. We feature student stories during presentations and on our social media accounts.

Our team loves sharing the joy of a child understanding new concepts. It allows our audience to experience firsthand the mission our team works towards every day; for students to maintain the same love of learning they brought to Kindergarten throughout all their years of schooling and into adulthood.

Thank you for being a loyal customer. We appreciate you!

The LtoJ Team

Follow us on Instagram, Facebook, TikTok and YouTube
@LtoJLLC

www.ingramcontent.com/pod-product-compliance
Lightning Source LLC
Chambersburg PA
CBHW081010120626
46546CB00010B/3098